Managing

I wish Ges had
ago when my fear of public speaking paralysed me...
Thankfully I found my voice but have so much still
to learn which is why this book is great—whether
you are starting out or wanting to improve the all-
important, though much feared, art and science of
speaking publicly.

Ges brings to life in great detail those feelings—
typically negative and both physical and emotional—
that so many of us experience when speaking in, or
even thinking about speaking in, public. In the same
way he brings to life (with his signature warmth,
humour and intellect) practical, detailed and step-
by-step explanations for those crucial components
needed to successfully open your talk.

Sukhi Jutia
Author and Entrepreneur

I carry this book with me to every speaking
engagement which gently reminds me to focus on
my breathing and posture. And most of all it feels like
I have a personal speaking coach to hand any time I
need it.

Mike Vacher
Director Nuffield Farming Scholarships Trust

A must for all those needing to speak in public. Ges
explains it is all about confidence and then goes on
to introduce techniques to enable you to hold the
attention of any audience. *Speak Performance* will
stay on my desk for good.

Julia Kirkland

Senior Partner Financial Services Training Partners

This book gives everyone who is apprehensive about speaking in public the tools to do so and is a must read for anyone getting on their feet and presenting for the first time.

Ellen Ross

Neuroscience Negotiator and Consultant

This is a new staple in my work bag!

Speak Performance isn't just a book about those huge TED style public speaking slots, but also for gut-wrenching networking introductions, nerve-inducing internal meetings and even uncomfortable one-on-one interactions...

This book is great to read cover to cover or to dip in and out of when needed. As someone who is used to public speaking, I was still amazed with the information provided in this guide and have taken on board the new techniques.

Nigel Biggs

Entrepreneur-in-Residence, Surrey University

Speak Performance is the first non-fiction book for years that I could not put down! Ges takes the reader, even if terrified of speaking in public, in gentle, positive and realistic steps towards achieving their aim. To be able to speak in a workplace presentation, in a networking group or (heaven forbid for most people) in public! This book is not about what you say but much more about how you prepare for and actually say it... Anybody asked to speak *in public* will benefit greatly and often from this short, snappy and super-supporting book.

SPEAK PERFORMANCE

How to be a confident, compelling and convincing speaker

Ges Ray

©2018 Ges Ray

First Published in Great Britain 2018 by mPowr (Publishing) Limited

www.mpowrpublishing.com

A catalogue record for this book is available from the British Library
ISBN – 978-1-907282-87-4

Cover Design and Illustrations by Martyn Pentecost
mPowr Publishing 'Clumpy™' Logo by e-nimation.com
Clumpy™ and the Clumpy™ Logo are trademarks of mPowr Limited

For Naj

My fiercest critic,
most ferocious supporter,
and friend for life...

Contents

Presenting:
You

The human brain starts working the moment you are born and never stops until you stand up to speak in public.

George Jessel

You're terrified.

Absolutely *terrified*.

Your heart is racing, you are breathing rapidly, breathing shallow, almost hyperventilating. Your mouth is dry, hands wringing wet, stomach churning, knees trembling, toes tingling, scrunched to the point where they hurt.

You've zoned out; haven't heard a word anyone else around you has said. You feel you are floating, almost in a parallel universe.

In this moment, hearing an explanation about fight-or-flight mechanisms, adrenaline, or your amygdala is the last thing on earth you want to hear.

In this moment, here is the last place on earth you want to be.

In this moment, if an escape hatch revealed itself, appeared in a far-flung corner of the last place on earth offering only a one-way trip to a distant universe, you'd seek it out, open it then jump through.

Why?

You are about to speak, that's why.

Not just speak, but speak in public. Public speaking. Not sitting comfortably, talking around a table–standing up and speaking in public.

Recognise these feelings?

Are you there now? In overwhelming fear?

Desperately trying to prepare a report for tomorrow, or for an internal meeting in a few hours. Yet the screen is swimming in front of your eyes, your fingers are feeling like sausages, too fat for the keyboard...

You feel you should have moved on from this. Moved on in life, moved on from these primeval feelings of distress, moved on from the sleepless nights. However, you have a presentation to prepare for that you are putting off until the last minute. Anything rather than reawaken that sense of foreboding that runs in parallel with waking up your presentation software program...

Everyone else considers you to be an experienced speaker, which is why you have been asked / requested / told to take that meeting, take that seminar, take to the stage to deliver a keynote at an event in the calendar, in the diary, on the horizon.

If truth be known, the horizon is where you would now prefer to be. You'd prefer to disappear over it rather than feel your confidence draining out of you as you make your way to the event.

So do something about it.

Something practical. Not theory, not explanations–ok, a few–but something that you can read, learn, mark and not only inwardly digest, but put into practice immediately.

Practical techniques that you can use in the office meeting in the morning, at the event in the afternoon.

Practical techniques drawn from many years of presenting, standing on stage as compère or MC, delivering workshops, even radio broadcasting.

Practical advice that–yes, with practice– builds your confidence to stand up and speak in public.

I make you a promise as you read this book.

The promise is that I will be your embarrassment sponge throughout. If there is a tumbleweed moment, a cringing I-wish-the-floor-would-open-up-and-swallow-me moment, I've probably been there and bought the T-shirt. I will describe in as much excruciating detail as I can, how nerves, fear and adrenaline affect you when speaking in public so that you can feel that embarrassment by association rather than experiencing it yourself, yet still learn from it, whilst building your confidence.

It's *all* about confidence.

And breathe...

You know the feeling.

You're at a business breakfast, networking. It's the 60-second round. In three people's time it's your turn; your turn to stand up and speak.

You're at an internal meeting, a board meeting. Your name is on the agenda. In three item's time the Chair will look at you; it's your turn to speak.

You're asked to say something at an event on your social calendar. A few words of thanks at a lunch, a poem or lesson at a friend's wedding. As you finish your coffee, you turn the page in the order of service. There it is; it's your turn to speak.

Freeze time for a moment. Look at what's happening.

How are you feeling?

The butterflies, awoken from their slumber, are flitting furiously around your stomach. There's a wonderful saying about never wanting to lose the butterflies, just have them flying in order, but in this case they have broken ranks. Right now they are performing aerial acrobatics worthy of an air show in the lurching space that you previously knew as your stomach.

Your mouth is dry; you wish you had a glass of water to hand but it's too late now.

Your hand is shaking. The previously pristine A4 sheet of paper with your notes is now all aquiver. (*Note to self*: next time use something smaller, something more stable, e.g. index cards.)

Whilst you are in that frozen moment of time, can you recall what was being said around the table or in the room for the preceding few minutes? Probably not; you've zoned out.

How do you feel? As if you've stepped through an opaque portal into that parallel universe. At this precise moment, you're none too keen to step back...

Whilst you've stopped time, rewind the clock to observe previous speakers, particularly at business events.

How often has someone started speaking before they've even got to their feet, got behind the chair, got to the front of the room? Started speaking, but soon ran out of breath? Soon found themselves almost gasping great gulps of air in order to simply get to the end?

What does this do for you, the speaker, and–just as importantly–what does this do for your audience?

For you, the speaker, you are indeed out of breath; few of us are as fit as we would like to be!

You're already in a state of high dudgeon as you walk up to the point in the room where you are due to speak. That trek–sometimes it feels like a trek–has just added to your distress.

You're breathing hard, your pulse rate has increased, you're a few degrees warmer than when you were sitting down, relaxed, a while ago. As for your warm, nervous hands... Let's just agree no one would want to shake your hand. Not just yet.

So why has this happened?

The fight-or-flight mechanism has kicked in. The adrenaline is flowing, you feel a great gulf of silence has opened up in front of you. You feel you simply must fill it with words, now, immediately, otherwise the audience will be on their feet leaving before you've even started...

That's not the case. Take a look now at what is really happening.

The people in front of you are likely to be warm, empathetic, looking forward to being informed, looking forward to being entertained. Unless of course you are unlucky enough to have a feral audience, which fortunately is rare.

When a speaker, particularly when it's one of our colleagues, is standing up in front of us looking out of sorts, looking nervous, we feel for them. We really feel for them. We *empathise* with them; thank heavens it's not us up there speaking! We also want to feel relaxed, feel comfortable in the presence of the speaker; we want to enjoy listening, want to enjoy being entertained.

We are also, on the whole, polite and courteous. We're adults after all. Age with maturity has given us that patina of politeness that masks the raw responses of the playground.

So when the speaker makes us feel uncomfortable we smile with encouragement, we clap our thanks, we nod to our neighbour. But we're not really listening. Our unspoken thoughts are urging that speaker to finish, urging that speaker to move on so we can be ready for the next voice.

Your pearls of wisdom are lost, cast into the sea of audience anxiety.

Here's what you can do about it.

Here's how can you take steps towards looking more confident. You're not going to lose the nerves, the anxiety, the adrenaline–well, not overnight at least–so here's what you can do to help the audience feel you are more confident, make the audience feel more relaxed, make the audience feel more disposed to want to listen to you.

Something practical, something essential, something fundamental.

Breathe.

How do you breathe? Or rather, how do you breathe when you are under pressure? How do you breathe when you arrive at the point in the room where you have to stand, have to face the audience, have to speak?

If at any point in your past you have been involved in amateur singing, amateur dramatics, even as far back as school, a few strands of memory may now be bubbling to the surface. Remember your conductor, your musical director, your teacher encouraging you to breathe properly, breathe deeply as you performed?

Why?

Breathing is fundamental to life. It provides your body with the oxygen you need to create energy. Breathing is vital to your very being; it is your life force. Without breath, you cease to exist.

Focus on your breathing for a moment. Listen to your breathing. Feel the air as you inhale, as you exhale. Watch your chest rise and fall.

How are you breathing now as you read this?

Chances are you are sitting reasonably comfortably, shallow breathing into the top of your lungs, the top of your chest.

I've probably made you think about it now. You are conscious of your breathing, whereas a minute or two ago it was absolutely automatic. Sorry about that! But we're going to make use of that awareness for a moment.

You're breathing now in relaxed mode, in comfortable mode, in the mode of most of your audience.

Look at what happens when you physically exert yourself, in sports, in the gym, or for some of us simply making it up the stairs... Yes, you breathe more quickly, but you automatically breathe more deeply, deeper into your lungs, deeper into your chest space.

Take this a step further, into the world of professional singers, professional athletes, professional speakers who have learned to make fuller use of their lung capacity.

When their musical director, coach or teacher urges them to "breathe deeply, breathe into your lower stomach, breathe in against

your ribcage, breathe into your back," it isn't a random instruction. It is simply an encouragement to make fuller use of their lung capacity.

Take this a step further; think of your automatic response when you *stop* breathing, when you're at risk of choking, of drowning. Imagine being in the water, in the underwater world of divers, in the deepwater world of freediving.

Imagine descending over 200 metres without equipment, without oxygen, underwater for over nine minutes fighting the urge to suck in great gulps of air... *(Warning! Don't try this in the bath at home...)*

How's your breathing now?

Practise this for yourself. Not freediving; I told you the bath isn't deep enough. Just breathing. When no one is looking(!), stand, and breathe normally. That's normal, relaxed, shallow breathing into the top of your lungs.

Now place the palm of your hand on your lower stomach, about hip height, or where–if you wear one–your belt buckle would be. As you breathe in, take the breath lower down into your lungs, down towards your hands, using that breath to push out against your hand.

Remember to breathe out again...

Now place your hands on your sides, palms against your lower ribcage, fingertips again about hip or belt high. As you breathe in, still breathing low down into your lungs, still pushing out against where your palm was a few moments ago on your lower stomach, now also push out sideways against your palms where they are now, at your sides on your lower ribcage.

Yes, remember to breathe out again!

Last exercise. Place your palms behind you, against your lower back, now at waist level, fingertips meeting at your spine.

As you breathe in deeply, still pushing against where your palm was on your lower stomach, still pushing against the sides of your ribcage, now also push against your hands where they are on your lower back.

Now you are breathing deeply...

Why focus on this?

Because when you're nervous, when you've rushed to the front of the room to speak, the risk is that your shallow breathing is what is seeing you through.

Those gasps, those gulps of air are being drawn at a fast and furious pace from your upper chest. That is how you can end up trapped in a vicious circle, fighting for survival, your breathing in control of you rather than you being in control of your breathing.

Seemingly unable to escape from a circle of shallow breathing, simply longing to finish so that you can get back to your seat and let the next person speak.

Guess what; your audience is feeling much the same.

So now you'll do something about it.

You've already pressed the pause button to freeze your moment of time; now press rewind to take you back to when you were sitting in the chair, waiting for your name to be called, waiting to speak.

The nerves are still there, the butterflies are still in air show acrobatic mode. Your hands are still quivering, palms still too damp to shake hands with anyone. That's not going to change.

What changes when you press replay is that when you reach the point in the room from whence you intend to speak, you're going to stop. Stop, then take a good deep breath before saying a word.

Just one good breath before you start.

Then begin speaking...

Press stop now. Look at the effect this has on you. Just as importantly, look at the effect this has on your audience.

For you as the speaker, this is what happens when you start with a good breath:

When you breathe deeply, you are making fuller use of your diaphragm, which is a dome-shaped muscle separating your chest from your abdomen. Not surprisingly, this is known as abdominal (or diaphragmatic) breathing. In itself this is more relaxing than emergency-mode breathing into the upper chest that is often part of the fight-or-flight response to stressful situations.

When you breathe deeply, with your diaphragm helping you to relax a fraction, your voice relaxes. Your voice drops a fraction as well, a few percentage points deeper, a few percentage points more authoritative.

When you breathe deeply, the pace of your delivery also drops a fraction. Taking the edge off the speed of your speaking has a double-whammy effect; as well as helping your audience better listen to you, better comprehend what you are saying, you also give yourself more time. Time to find the right words, time to deliver a more comprehensive message rather than the garbled torrent of words from a rushed opening.

Note the emphasis on fractions and degrees here. This is about the principle of marginal gains, not dramatic changes or Damascene revelations. By tweaking the performance of each element of your speaking, with practice and rehearsal you build your skills, build yourself into a more effective speaker.

So now return to your audience, still in their seats, eagerly awaiting your pearls of wisdom. See what effect your deep breath has had on them. Feedback on you as the speaker could include:

- They felt more confident in you from the outset, more relaxed, more willing to listen to you rather than feeling anxious on your behalf

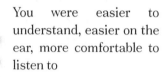

- You were easier to understand, easier on the ear, more comfortable to listen to

- They were more able to listen, more able to take on board, more able to comprehend your opening statements, rather than only really getting to grips with what you were saying as you got into your stride a few lines in

In essence, you have just established a handshake with your audience. A good, firm, warm, confident handshake. Just as when you meet someone for the first time with a warm, firm greeting. A warm, firm handshake that sets the scene for the rest of your presentation, whilst you're only a few seconds in.

Yet all you did was take a good, deep breath.

Your standing in the community

How's your standing with your audience? Rephrase that; how's your standing?

We are talking about your handshake with the audience, a firm, confident, inviting handshake that helps to immediately establish a warm rapport with the people in the room. You will now build on the breathing to add something straightforward to your opening few seconds.

How do you stand? When you arrive at that point in the room at which you will turn around to face your audience, what stance will you take? Not as in what side of the argument are you on as you begin (although that may be having an effect on how nervous you feel!), but what will you look like to your audience?

For a moment, take your mind back to presentations you have experienced where the speaker has made you feel uncomfortable on their account. Look at what happens when the nerves and adrenaline strike. Put yourself in their shoes. Look at what happens for the audience; look at what happens for you as the speaker.

Can you identify with the speaker who wears out the carpet as they talk? Perfectly understandable; they've had a rush of primeval energy, it needs to dissipate. Moving as you talk can help your audience better understand your message, but so often that energy comes out as a nervous jiggle, or a tight, contorted position as you stand flamingo-like on one leg maybe, or hands, knees, everything in awkward positions.

Here's the impact on your audience. Again, you're sending signals of nervousness, transmitting a feeling that you are uncomfortable. Guess what? Your wonderful, warm, empathetic audience are again feeling uncomfortable on your behalf.

Think about the impact on you, the speaker. For a moment, imagine a virtual reality headset enables you to step outside your earthly body whilst presenting; turn around, observe what is happening.

Take a good old-fashioned Sherlock Holmes magnifying glass. Examine your doppelganger self for the one part of you without which you would not be able to communicate any message...

Your voice.

First of all, have you ever looked at your voice? I mean *really* looked at your voice? How your voice works?

If you've ever seen one of the YouTube videos where the camera slips down the throat, you may agree that this is not something to watch over breakfast... If the idea of watching mucous membranes stretched over your larynx, vibrating, has no appeal, then you are on safer ground calling up a diagram instead, as that is what your voice is. Vibrating mucous membranes sitting, like a gyroscope, in your throat.

Your voice is amazing.

What makes your voice unique is the way you use resonating chambers; your chest space, your head spaces, your soft palate, to deliver the sound. Part of what makes the difference between a voice that comes out tight, comes out strangled, against a voice that can reach the back of the room is the way you position yourself to enable those resonating chambers to work. (Warming up this incredible instrument also helps...)

For now, focus on delivering as strong, as confident a voice as you are able in this opening audience handshake.

For now, focus on how holding yourself more confidently, how standing firmly, how standing securely can help achieve this at least for your opening few seconds. Agreed, you don't want to be a pillar of salt for the entire presentation; here you are simply working on your initial impression.

Saying, "Just stand properly," doesn't really help. So here's a straightforward technique that is easy to remember.

Using your imagination, bring to mind an image, a feeling, a moment that represents the ideas of solid, immovable, not-going-to-budge-in-a-millennium. It may be a memory from holiday, a favourite walk, something you work with.

Using any more descriptors at this point risks overriding your imagination, so hold on to whatever slips into your mind now; work with that.

A few examples are mentioned below if you are really stuck, but it's best if you work with your own thoughts.

A personal input here, with the image that I use together with its origins. One of the reasons behind why I do what I do now, building your confidence in public speaking, is because more years ago than I care to remember I was encouraged to join a management training organisation, the British Junior Chamber of Commerce.

As a young bank clerk en route to becoming a bank manager, saying no was simply not an option. Seemingly within milliseconds I was taking part in public speaking competitions, admittedly not altogether willingly. Part of the training process was exactly this exercise, and for me the image of an oak tree still works. Even now, many years later, thinking of that tree helps relax the knees, taking some of the tension out of the legs.

In client workshops, the ideas have ranged from a mountain view on holiday to a cathedral on a hill, an industrial vehicle to a horse standing in a field...

Take the output from your own imagination. Bring it to mind as you stand in front of your own audience. Just for a second or two, use whatever works for you to help you stand securely, stand with more confidence.

Now speak.

Here's what's been achieved.

For you, the speaker, you have again tweaked a performance element, made another marginal improvement in your speaking through enabling your voice to perform more to its potential. We all want to hear a rich, mellifluous, confident voice; you've made a step towards that. You are also standing more confidently, not wearing out the carpet, not contorting yourself into nervous positions.

For your audience, beginning by holding yourself in a more confident manner, beginning with a more confident stance, beginning with a more confident voice, you have helped with *their* confidence in you as a speaker. They are marginally more comfortable, more ready, indeed more willing to listen.

You have already established a warmer, firmer handshake, yet you're still only a couple of seconds in...

Here's looking at you

You've established a handshake with your audience. A warm, firm, confident handshake. So far so good, but you are still only a few seconds in; now you need to capture their attention.

How do you do that?

Here's an action you take as a matter of course in day-to-day life, but which tends to get forgotten when the adrenaline is rushing...

Put it in context first. You meet someone for the first time, you extend that warm, firm, confident handshake, then you automatically... look at them. It's how we communicate, it's how we gauge our welcome, gauge the reaction.

Would you gaze past their right ear into the distance?

No, of course not. Similarly, if you are on the receiving end of a handshake, you would look in askance at the other party if they did not meet your gaze.

You're with friends for a coffee catch-up in the café, with colleagues in the pub, round the table with your family. You've got the juiciest piece of gossip to impart, you're first with the news, eyes shining with excitement as the story almost bursts out of you!

Would you be gazing out of the window as you thrilled your audience? No. Automatically, in the moment, you would be sharing your gaze as you shared your story, bringing everyone in. "Listen! This is really interesting!" is the message your eyes are sending.

Now move to your office, to work, to the business environment. It's all so last minute.

It's now the end of the day; you realise that at 9:15 in the morning you have to present to a meeting. You are nothing if not diligent, so thoughts are thunk, jewels jotted, bullet points bulleted. Job done. You're as prepared as you'll ever be.

Next morning you're on your feet, notes tucked comfortingly in your hand, or discreetly laid to one side on a lectern or the edge of a convenient table.

Yet, wishing to look more professional, you picture them in your mind rather than look at the notes. As you earnestly work through your beautifully bullet-pointed pearls of wisdom from that mental checklist, it's easy–indeed strangely comforting–to look at that light fitting or picture on the wall whilst running though points one, two, three, four...

Stop!

You've lost them. In fact you probably lost them a few seconds in.

If you had slammed your hand down on to the table at that point–I know you wouldn't, you're far too respectful, but bear with

me—and if you asked those in the room what were they thinking, exactly what were they really, honestly thinking at that very moment, a good percentage would admit they had drifted off.

Drifted off into that alternative universe of random in-the-moment thoughts that seems to sit alongside us when we're trying to work. "When's the next coffee break? Why didn't I grab a coffee on the way in? What's for lunch? What's in the fridge at home for this evening? Did I inject the cat?"

OK, that last one is my own. Our last remaining cat is very elderly, very deaf, also diabetic. So twice a day I have to grab her by the scruff of the neck to inject a dose of insulin. Twice-daily injections are an essential part of the household routine, so "Did I inject the cat?" is one of those random domestic thoughts that slides into view when I'm not paying full attention.

Smartphones have left us dumb humans with such a short attention span that it's easy to forget what you were going to say.

Your audience is no different; add a warm room, or a speaking slot just after lunch. The need to grab their attention is all the more imperative.

Or the complete opposite. You walk into the room to an audience of strangers. Amongst the sea of unfamiliar faces is a colleague. "Thank heavens, I've got a friend!" is the unconscious message in your head. Before you know it, you've delivered almost all the presentation to one person, your friend.

Even though you've eyeballed them non-stop, you've missed the signals that said, "Would you please look away? Look somewhere else. I'm beginning to feel really uncomfortable." They may no longer be your friend by the end...

So here's what you should do.

To state the obvious, yes, look at your audience, but put a bit of structure behind that. Then consider from a business perspective why you should make the effort, why you should rehearse the technique of including everyone in your sight line. Then look at accommodating the range of room shapes, the range of room sizes that you are likely to encounter.

Structure first of all. Not suggesting a methodical, numbers-driven process. You wouldn't allocate a defined, methodical time slot to each set of eyes at a water cooler moment when you have a juicy snippet of gossip to share.

What you would do, automatically, is take your gaze around the group, enthusiastically capturing attention, holding the gaze a little longer with anyone who had slipped away from your story (how dare they!), ensuring your message had been delivered.

Now do the same with your audience. Practise capturing their attention so that it becomes as automatic here as in the moment over coffee.

So why should you put in the effort? Surely you're reaching most of them? Surely you're ok to reach 80%?

Pareto's Law, the 80/20 rule, has a reach beyond the world of sales funnels; apply it here. Unless you are very fortunate indeed, in most audiences there will be only a small core of people whom either you are targeting directly, or who may be interested enough in what you are saying to speak with you over a follow-up coffee or in the bar afterwards.

But only if you've caught their attention.

What a waste if, after all your efforts, you find that crucial core had been dispersed around tables in the extremes of the room. After all your efforts, you hadn't drawn them into the conversation...

Which segues neatly into the shape of the room, the dispersal of the tables around us.

In a small meeting room, with everyone comfortably in sight as you rise from your chair, this is not too much of a problem. Just remember to engage all the eyes; job done.

Now scale up the room; it's a business breakfast meeting with tables to the left of you, tables to the right of you. More than just remembering to engage eyes, you must make the effort to pay extra attention to the people in the margin of your range of vision, make the effort to deliberately look far left, look far right.

Scale up again. You're now at an event, in a hall, speaking from stage, the numbers have risen from the tens to the hundreds. Throw in stage lights obscuring the audience.

Your ability to see the eyes of more than a few rows has now diminished, yet there is an increased requirement on you as the speaker to make the effort to engage, an increased requirement to make the effort to reach the sea of eyes that you cannot see.

Even for your audience in the balcony, by looking up in their direction you are helping to make an emotional connection.

Even if you do have that (rare!) feral audience, you have at least cranked up the chances of making that one connection that makes the event worthwhile.

Even if something goes wrong when you are presenting to a room or on stage–which it will–you are in a better place to recover because you have engaged. Your audience is *with* you rather than just looking *at* you.

All you have done is what you would do as a matter of course when in that café, in that pub, round that table. All you have done is use your eyes to draw your audience into the conversation.

All you have to do now is practise so that it becomes just as natural when you are speaking in public.

Now to add something to that....

May fortune smile upon you

It's a wonderful day.

Dream of coffee. Or hot chocolate. Whatever it is that you look forward to grabbing a cup of before the meeting.

It's a good day; you're on time. So much so you have time to grab a cup from the coffee shop just round the corner. It's an even better day; two baristas are waiting to serve you!

Who do you like to do business with?

One barista clearly got out of bed the wrong side that morning, had a row with their partner, their goldfish and some poor random commuter on the way to work. They grimace at you with a face that looks like it's sucking a hairball soaked in vinegar. The other welcomes you warmly with a wonderful smile.

Which one are you drawn to? Which one do you want to do business with?

Out of the café now; move into the workplace. It's the same morning, you're at the meeting, you're due to give a presentation to a key audience. When you're presenting, what face do you present? Or should that be what face does your audience see? Hairball soaked in vinegar or a warm, engaging smile?

No trick questions here, simply something that is natural, automatic in day-to-day life, yet has a tendency to sneak out by the back door when you stand up to speak.

Sometimes it's the nerves, sometimes it's the audience, sometimes simply that feeling that you have to be serious in order to be businesslike. Quite understandable. Having once been a bank manager, I appreciate that when dealing with fellow professionals in say accountancy or legal services, there is a need for a touch of gravitas.

Rewind to when you greeted people as they walked into the room. Along with that warm, firm handshake, along with looking at them, you smiled.

That's what we all do. It's part of our greeting, part of our engagement. No matter whether it is new contacts in a social setting, or those same accountancy and legal professionals, unless you had deliberately set out to be stern, to be severe, the chances are you exchanged a smile as part of your warm greeting.

Did you know that smiling changes the way your audience hears your voice? If you have heard it said that a smiley voice is more effective on the telephone, this is not simply folklore, it is grounded in truth, for reasons that are more physiological than psychological.

When you smile, the soft palate at the back of your throat lifts, which helps the sound waves become more fluid. If you sing in a choir, or just in the car or the shower(!), the encouragement you have been given to take the sound into your soft palate is for good reason; it helps the voice to sound warmer, sound friendlier, sound receptive.

So what has this to do with public speaking?

One of my favourite quotes is from the American poet, Maya Angelou:

"I've learned that people will forget what you said, people will forget what you did, but people will never forget how you made them feel."

Quickly remember then rattle off the three best talks or presentations that you've been to recently. No analysis, just the ones that pop into your mind now. What made them make the cut?

Yes, of course the content is important. Of course the slides matter. But I'll lay odds that an important factor was how the speaker made you feel. How the speaker made you, as an individual, feel engaged, feel welcome.

There's an old wives' tale around using more muscles to frown than smile, so don't go there. What is less disputed is that smiling, even when you don't feel like it, lifts the mood, slows the heart rate, reduces the perceived level of stress, sending signals to the rest of our body that all is OK.

It's a double whammy; smiling builds audience engagement and makes us feel better about ourselves.

Two practical exercises for you:

1. When you are next talking with a group of friends in the café, the bar, over a drink, deliberately throw in a smile or two. Note the reaction. There's a good chance a chunk of your audience will smile back at you automatically. It's what we all do...

2. When you next have to stand up to present, make the effort to open with a smile. As you catch the eyes of your audience, add in a few more. Agreed, it may feel a little odd or false to you as the speaker. Agreed, you don't want to be grinning like a Cheshire cat if a warm smile is not your natural disposition, so get there by degrees. If you have a trusted colleague in the audience, ask for feedback. You may be surprised....

To recap.

You've covered two techniques to help build that warm, opening handshake with your audience; how you breathe, how you stand.

You've reminded yourself of a couple of normal, human interactions that help you engage with people. Interactions that tend to get forgotten when the nerves and adrenaline strike; simply remembering to look, remembering to smile at people.

Yet you've only just begun!

You now want to hold your audience's attention, so here's something that will help them stay with you.

Nothing is more revealing than movement.

Martha Graham (dance choreographer)

You are lined up to present in the meeting tomorrow. One of many speakers; it's busy, a lot of ground to cover.

The agenda has just arrived; you scan quickly to check your time slot. Sadly, no mistake. It's fourth in a row just before the coffee break. You know with a sinking heart that coffee is the only thing you would be focusing on if you were to be in the audience at that moment. What could be worse?

Well, at least you are not first on after a snatched sandwich or sticky sweet-laden business lunch; you can already see the glazed eyes doing their politest best to stay awake a few minutes in.

Or should that be glazed *eye*–in the singular– as its pair is already closed behind a carefully placed hand? The owner of which feels they are doing a pretty good job of disguising their dozing; not realising that most of the room are adopting similar body language...

Here's what you can do about it. The lottery of speaking slots within the day's agenda is a nightmare for speakers. If you are fortunate enough to have a say in your preferences you would of course avoid the pre-coffee / immediate post-lunch slots, but often that's not the case. Having a technique up your sleeve that can help maintain your audience's attention, help your audience more easily register and remember what you are saying, comes in useful here.

How do you move on stage? Indeed, have you considered moving when on stage? No, you don't need to take to the dance floor (although that would definitely get their attention even after the heaviest of lunches!), but how about planning ahead to make best use of whatever space you have available?

If your natural reserve is already causing you to register red on the cringe factor spectrum, making you feel you are tempted to skip the next bit and jump to the next chapter, bear with me.

Here's a typical scenario for a business presentation. The room is boardroom layout, with a screen at one end, in front of which you will be standing to deliver your piece.

Or move up a notch. You are in a larger room with chairs in theatre style or banquet tables, with a raised stage area complete with screen, perhaps with a lectern already waiting for you. Waiting for you to head towards it, spin round and speak from that point.

Or will you?

If your priority to date has been to simply get up, get it over with, then get back to your chair you will not be alone. Many others in the room will feel the same. So now we'll again work on a marginal gain, a differential that could add a margin of effectiveness that can set you apart from other speakers in today's meeting.

When you make your move from your chair to the front of the room you have a choice.

You can head for the place from whence the other speakers have delivered. Be just the same as them. *Or* you can plan to make use of the space available to be more effective.

If this were a theatre workshop, we would be talking about blocking the stage. For actors, this means working out where to move, where to stand for the most dramatic effect in delivering their lines. Working out sight lines for the audience, making best use of the lighting design, best use of the scenery.

Yes, I hear you; you're not a nascent thespian, you simply want to be a better business speaker. But think for a moment about TEDx talks.

Why does the *TEDx Organiser Guide* go into such detail about designing the experience, designing the stage... if not to help speakers give their audience a better experience?

So for your next presentation, if there is space available, make use of it.

Very simply, whether in the boardroom environment or on the stage, look to deliver your first key message from one side of the screen. Then, resisting the urge to walk'n'talk, move to the other side of the screen to deliver your next message, clicking the clicker if this is the right time to change slide.

With this one movement, you have delivered multiple outcomes:

- When you deliver a message from one point in the room, your audience is registering person one, delivering message one, from position one. That message is parcelled up; associated with that point in the room

- By then moving to another part of the room, you help your audience in dealing with a fresh message. You become person two, delivering message two, from point two

You are helping your audience stay attentive by signposting that a new message is coming up.

If you are using slides, that non-speaking moment as you click the clicker whilst walking to presenting point two gives your audience a few useful moments to take on board the new slide content. You also avoid that otherwise awkward moment when you are trying to talk, whilst they are trying to simultaneously listen and read the slide. Usually nobody wins...

Rinse and repeat. Here you have a fundamental, yet effective technique to help keep your audience with you throughout your presentation, help them remember the points you are making.

Of course this is not the sole preserve of slide-based presentations. One caveat is that sometimes you will be in a restricted environment, perhaps only able to stand behind your chair, where movement is either impossible or ridiculous.

Sometimes though by looking at the room with fresh eyes before you speak, you can mentally block the room in the same way that actors would with their stage.

Work out where to move, where to stand, for a more effective delivery.

Last but not least, where are you now on the cringe factor this-isn't-for-me spectrum? What is stopping you from trying this out? What is stopping you from starting with baby steps, at your next presentation?

Presenting:
Your Voice

You don't hear what I hear.

Lailah Gifty Akita

We've all been there. In a meeting, a company presentation, a conference. Fighting to keep at least one eyelid open, zoning out as the speaker drones on, and on, in the same soporific tone. It's the very definition of monotonous; a voice that is unchanging in pitch, a voice without intonation.

How does this make the audience feel? How does this make *you* feel when you are that audience?

But now it's you that's speaking; now it's you that has drawn the short straw for that post-lunch graveyard slot. Now it's you facing a sea of faces with the potential to all have one eyebrow raised as the other droops towards sleep.

How can you avoid being that monotonous, soporific speaker? How can you help your audience to better understand the message that you are delivering? How can you help them stay awake?

Let's explore how you use your voice.

Your voice is an amazing instrument. In the course of a normal working day you deliver important messages, tell stories, mention something that affects you, automatically selecting a voice tone that reflects the message.

If your voice were the gearbox in an automatic vehicle, you wouldn't even have to think about using the gear selector; your voice would be in the appropriate gear without much input from you.

Yet when you stand up to speak, to address a meeting, to deliver a presentation with heart racing, with adrenaline flowing, it's easy for that automatic voice tone selection ability to switch off now that you are *public speaking*.

You're now learning to drive a manual voice gearbox, where—at least to start with—you have to select the voice tone that is appropriate to the terrain. Remember when you first started driving? Finding the right gear for the right circumstances took time, took effort, yet after a while you forgot about changing gear because it became an automatic action.

That is what has happened for you in your normal working day; your voice selects the voice tone to reflect the message without you having to think about it. That's what you want to work towards with your public speaking voice.

But why bother?

Why put this effort in to do anything about it?

Here's the driver.

The driver is your business. To be more effective when you stand up to speak, to have more impact, to reach more of your audience. The driver is more business.

In this section, we will look at five voice tones, how you use them in normal life, with straightforward techniques for making them automatically part of your public speaking voice gearbox.

Silence is golden, golden.

The Four Seasons – Silence is Golden 1964

There is a voice that is the most powerful, the most effective voice of all.

The voice of silence.

Only a short while ago you were probably talking with friends or colleagues as part of your normal day. What consideration did you give to the rate at which you were speaking, the rate at which the listeners' brains could absorb what you were saying, the ability of your audience to take on board the points you were making together with everything else going on around them?

Probably none. The conversation likely had a natural ebb and flow, with pauses occurring where they needed to, for dramatic effect or for you to take a sip of a drink. You didn't need to think about it at all.

Now it's all changed. Now you are standing up to speak to an audience with those two companions of public speaking, nerves and adrenaline, firmly in attendance.

First of all, let's look at the effect on you as the speaker, then the impact on your audience.

As the speaker, as you walk up to the front of the room, you've again just stepped into what feels like a parallel universe. Your heart rate is up, your heat rate is up, your sweat rate is up!

You wish you hadn't worn such a warm outfit today. That smart heavyweight dress, that immaculate thick wool jacket seemed perfect in the cool of the morning, but right at this moment you wish it came with an integral miniature air conditioning unit...

Dress is not a topic for now, yet planning what outfit to wear when speaking can be important because *you are on fire*! Key points at the ready, slides moving, messages being delivered in salvoes. How could they fail to be impressed, fail to listen?

Well. They could.

Whilst loathe to break this to you, take a step back for a moment. Stop time again. Take a look at your audience. Observe their body language as they sit comfortably, sit relaxed, sit with arms folded. Or rest on one elbow twirling a pen 'twixt the fingers. They are still on Planet Earth, feet firmly fixed on terra firma, having failed to make the stellar journey with you into your speaker's universe.

The responsibility lies with you as the speaker to bring your rocket-fuelled pace of delivery back down to earth, to provide your audience with space and time. Surely you want your listeners to hear what you are saying? To take on board the points you are making? Otherwise, what is the point in your being there?

The responsibility lies with you to give your audience the time to hear what has been said. To use moments of silence, to break up your delivery so that your audience can process, can understand the content, then be ready to move on with you to the next point.

Better this than your audience having to play constant catch-up. Turning to a neighbour whilst muttering, "What did they say?"

Giving your audience time to listen, time to absorb will help lift their retention rate, also help them better engage with you.

Whilst the time button is on pause, take a fresh look at your comfortable, relaxed audience. Take a fresh look at their ability to fail to listen to you–oh, the temerity!–even when you are still speaking.

Think of the last time, probably not so long ago, when you wished the speaker had repeated a key point or number because at that precise moment your mind was somewhere else. Perhaps it was you that had to turn to a neighbour whilst muttering, "What did they say?"

As an audience member, it's not your fault. You have a remarkable brain that has the ability to continuously process information. Process the words of the speaker, process the activity in the room around you, process your own thoughts.

As a speaker, however, it is your responsibility to be aware that your audience do have remarkable brains with the ability–even when you are speaking–to drift off. To think about the next coffee break, what's for lunch, what's in the fridge, did the cat get injected?

If the parallel universe analogy seems a little far-fetched, here's a more real-world example of what can feel like a time difference between speaker and audience. To illustrate, here's a question to which I hope the answer will be no, but bear with me.

Have you ever had the experience of being the driver of a vehicle or motor bike in a relatively dramatic crash?

Having personally experienced both, I can still run in my head the slow-motion film of those few seconds before the collision.

For those of you for whom the answer is yes, I can see you nodding your heads in agreement at how time seems to slow down in those few seconds before the impact as the adrenaline rushes.

For those for whom the answer is no, I hope the majority, please again bear with me as I describe the motorcycle incident.

One of my business development roles after moving on from the bank involved a daily commute by train to London, the wrong side of two hours each way. Several of my colleagues came in by motorbike. As the weather warmed into Spring, it seemed an obvious route to pursue. After a week's holiday spent on a direct access course, I was the proud holder of a full motorcycle licence.

Two days after that I was an even prouder owner of a thumping great 650cc single cylinder BMW that was perfect for commuting; slim upright frame, ABS brakes, with acceleration that took your breath away. Forty-five minutes saved each way with a journey that was now fun, if challenging; job done.

All went well until trundling (within the speed limit of course) down the A3 one day, when a lorry pulled out of a side turning to cross the carriageway in front of me.

The driver had seen the clear patch of road; the driver had not seen me.

We're a few seconds away from my bike slamming into the side of the lorry; a few seconds from proving the worth of wearing full leathers even in the height of Summer, a few seconds from proving the worth of investing in a top-quality helmet.

The bike, ABS full on, is quivering as it does its best to stop, but to no avail. In seconds, the bike and its rider are scattered across the road.

The film of that incident I can still run in my head. It is way, way longer than a few seconds. The surge of adrenaline has a contrary effect on the internal time clock, seemingly allowing enough time even after slamming the brakes on to brew a pot of tea, pour it, stir it, allow it to cool then drink it, all before the collision.

Allowing enough time to whistle a happy tune, right to the end....

OK, a tad overdramatic when we're talking about your next meeting or presentation, which I'm sure will not be a car-crash moment, but when you next see a movie where the film slows down time at the denouement, think of this as an example. An example of the difference 'twixt you and your audience, an example of the feeling of a time difference.

You, fuelled with nerves, fuelled with adrenaline, potentially rattling off at a rate of knots, feeling that every gap between the words is a great gulf of time that has to be filled, otherwise they will not only be thinking of a cup of tea they will leave the room to put the kettle on.

Then there's your audience. Who are not fuelled with anything other than tea or coffee. Those unique beverages that enable your audience to make full use of their multi-processing ability to think of other things whilst you speak, unless you do something about it.

So here's what you can do about it.

Practical steps you can put in place to use the silent voice more effectively to keep your audience on board.

Firstly, recognise that as a speaker being silent you have to overcome embarrassment. Overcome the embarrassment of moments when you are saying absolutely nothing, yet all the eyes are looking at you.

Secondly, recognise that it is easy to sit here, easy to read this, easy to nod in agreement. Easy on paper to work through the reasons why this helps both you and your audience. Easy to rationalise use of this voice and reinforce why you should use it. Easy to then do nothing about it.

Thirdly, recognise that nothing beats putting the theory into practice, helping it become another gear that you automatically select.

So baby steps, starting with the ones below:

- Breathing. Revisit the steps you worked through in the first chapter. Get used to taking that good breath before you speak. A comfortable breath when you reach the natural end of a sentence, when you've made a key point. Just as you would if talking with colleagues or with friends around the table.

- Similarly, remember to smile, remember to look at your audience at those junctures. These natural responses help you look more comfortable at the front of the room when not speaking.

- When putting together your notes, your script, your plan, mark up the places at which you want the audience to accept the point you have made. Or the point at which you move to the next topic. Make it clear for yourself that here is where you will pause, here is where you will break, here is where you will use silence.

- Rehearse using the pauses, using the moments of silence. Not just from the timing point of view, but to get used to the feeling of not speaking at the end of that sentence. Back to our public speaking voice gearbox again; if you haven't got used to the feeling of slipping smoothly through neutral to reach point three, you are more likely to crunch the synchromesh on the way through.

- If possible, rehearse in front of those who will afford you constructive, unbiased feedback. Specifically ask about the length of the pause. (Yes, I agree, immediate family are not always constructive or unbiased!) You may be surprised at what for you felt *forever*, elicits a response along the lines of a shrug of the shoulders with the comment, "Hardly noticed it."

- If not, record yourself via your phone or other device, then when replaying take the role of an audience member. Put aside the fact that you dislike hearing your own voice; take an objective view on how long it takes to receive and understand what is being said before you are ready to move on.

Remember, a moment of silence does not have to mean you stand stock-still on stage with a rictus grin. Taking an unhurried sip of water, checking your notes, moving to another part of the stage as you change the slide, these are all actions that give you cover whilst not speaking, at least until you are comfortable with using silence.

So here's what has been achieved for you, perhaps more importantly for your audience, by deliberately using silence.

For you, a means to tell your story, to get your points across. To speak in a less frantic fashion.

Guess what. You will be better understood.

A bonus, which shines through time and time again in workshops, is the extra time that you have in your back pocket. Time to put your thoughts in order, to be more coherent. Time to hear, time to clock, time to pick up on other conversation references within the room.

For your audience, you have given them the time to listen to those coherently delivered pearls of wisdom. The time to process them.

The time to acknowledge them, the time to be ready to move on with you to the next point.

All this, yet when you think about it, you haven't said a word.

You've simply been silent.

The more faithfully you listen to the voices within you, the better you will hear what is sounding outside.

Dag Hammarskjold

Former Secretary-General of the United Nations

Think back to the last time you were entertained; *really* entertained. Heart-thumping, gut-wrenching, tear-jerking, back-of-the-seat entertainment. Live theatre, cinema, concert hall, VR headset; whatever floats your boat.

Think now about *how* you were entertained. Strip out the CGI animation, the costumes, the music, the lights.

What are you left with?

Voices. You're left with only the voices.

Your voice has the power to entertain.

Have you had the privilege of attending a local TEDx event? Or watched a TEDx talk? Or it's bigger brother, TED? If so, you may be aware that TED stand for Technology, Entertainment and Design.

That's *entertainment*, not education. We all want to be entertained when listening to a talk or presentation, within either or both of these definitions:

entertain

verb:

1. provide (someone) with amusement or enjoyment

2. give attention or consideration to (an idea or feeling)

To equip you with the power to entertain, here are four more voice tones. Four voice tones within the range that you use naturally in day-to-day life, but which easily desert you when standing up to speak to that room, that conference, with the added pressure of having to feel you are businesslike.

Voice tones that will help your presentation be more entertaining, help your presentation better engage with your audience.

The power is in your voice.

Mechanically, your vocal folds, or cords, are a couple of bits of mucous membrane, stretched across the larynx, which vibrate.

Physically, that's all they are, sitting like a gyroscope in your throat. But with exponential

potential to add warmth, flavour and colour to help you deliver entertainment rather than just a collection of words.

Here you are going to look more closely at straightforward techniques for making these voices part of your public speaking toolkit.

For each voice I will describe a scenario, something you do in normal life. I will demonstrate what happens when the nerves strike. We will then look at fundamental, practical exercises you can use to find those voices, exercises that you can do where you are right now, as you read this.

OK, right now might not be entirely appropriate; if you are on the train or within sight of your work colleagues you may not feel entirely comfortable in talking to yourself or waving your arms around! So bear with me, mark the page, then make a note for when you and I can talk 1-2-1...

Voices in your head?
Tell me your story.

Here's that same scenario again. You've got the most amazing, juicy, hot-off-the-press story to tell. You're in the café sharing a coffee or in the bar with your friends, round the table with your family, or grabbing a drink in the office kitchen with your colleagues.

Do-you-say-it-in-a-flat-mono-tone-voice? No, of course you don't. Apart from anything else, you'd soon be trumped by someone else's story! You're grinning with anticipation, your eyes are shining, your, "Hey, listen to this!" is almost delivered from your eyes as you bubble over with excitement.

That's the head voice, the voice for stories. In normal life you would automatically take your voice up into your head, up into the cavity that resonates with excitement. So when you want to catch your audience's attention, impart exciting new information, tell a story about your business, why shouldn't you do the same?

Now find that voice.

Exercise

Here's a practical exercise to help find that story voice.

First, though I'll remind you of my promise. You didn't notice, but I rehearsed all these exercises in the room just a few moments before you read this, so I have extracted all the embarrassment from the room for you. I am your embarrassment sponge; you are free to feel suave, feel sanguine, feel sophisticated.

So OK to join in the exercise? Deal? Shake hands?

Excellent. Now that you and I have a verbal contract to proceed, we'll begin.

You are going to make a *whoop* sound.

Yes, you did hear me correctly; a whoop sound. Flash back to your childhood when something really exciting had happened. So exciting you couldn't contain your enthusiasm! That is where we are going.

We recognise that natural, infectious, unaffected enthusiasm when we hear it in others because the voice is resonating in the head, in the chambers, in the cavities and cheekbones.

We still do it as adults when the moment takes us. You've just come back from the most *amazing* holiday... The views were *incredible*... Listen to yourself as you tell the story; feel the sound rising up into your head space.

Now replicate the childhood excitement, the adult enthusiasm with a *whoop!*

Start from a normal speaking voice, then lift the sound into the cheekbones, into the eyes, up to the top of the head, eyes widening as you relive something amazing!

Whooo-oooop!

That's the head voice, the excited story voice. That's what we used as a child at the drop of a hat before those crippling agents *awareness* and *embarrassment* crept into our lives.

As adults, that's what we use when we are in comfortable company when we are carried away with the passion of the moment.

So now put yourself in the shoes of your audience, listening to you talking about your business. What is going to catch your interest? Hold your attention? A flat, monotonous delivery?

Or a speaker whose eyes shine with the excitement that is also being reflected in the voice that resonates with the top of the *whoop* that recalls our own experiences of excitement?

That's the head voice. For stories.

Why shouldn't you tell exciting stories about your business?

Listen! This is important! I need to get it off my chest.

Here's scenario two. You're the captain / team leader, the game is going, shall we say, less than well; there are things-to-be-said at half-time. I'd suggest you will probably not be speaking in either a-flat-mono-tone-voice, or an excited story voice. No. I can see you now;

confident stance, powerful delivery, message clear, message understood.

Switch that scenario now to your board / team meeting, where you have a key message to deliver. It's the same. What's your message? What message will your team hear if that key statement is delivered in flat-mono-tone delivery? What impact will your opening statement have if, thanks to nerves, your colleagues hear it in a squeakier voice than your normal pitch ?

Your opening handshake with your audience sets the platform for the message you want to deliver. This can be a firm, strong, effective handshake that sets the tone from the outset.

Or a weaker, not-the-best-of-first-impressions handshake that you then have to recover from once you've got into your stride.

Your choice. Here's a practical exercise to help you find your chest voice.

I promise, no more whoops.

Exercise

I'm taking you into your kitchen, to one of the corner cupboards.

Yes, you heard me correctly. Into your kitchen. Don't worry; I'm not expecting a show kitchen from the marketing suite of a new housing development, all pristine, all perfect, so there's no need for that moment of alarm or to rush in for a clean-up. The best kitchen for this exercise is the real one that you live in with cupboards full of bits and bobs that you've accumulated over time.

Reach into the back of the cupboard for one of those jars that you've put away at the back after a celebration, one of those jars of pickle left over from Christmas. Or of course use your imagination if you are on the train or reading this in your coffee shop! It's a jar that has been opened then put back a few times, acquiring that slightly sticky, difficult to open quality. Or if that makes you shudder, then it's one of those brand-new jars, tricky to open first time round.

Now bring the jar (real or imaginary) down to chest level, one hand on the lid, one hand on the base of the jar. Put some effort into twisting off that tough lid. Go on, twist! Throw in a few grunts! *Really* put some effort in!

Now stop. Freeze mid-twist.

Feel where the tension is across your chest, your upper arms; a band of tension around your torso.

That's where your chest voice comes from.

Before you move on, an addendum to that exercise. I'll add another image, another flavour to help reinforce the feeling of where this key voice is located. Flavour is very relevant here, as you again journey into your kitchen, into your cupboard to reach for another jar.

What other sticky-lidded jars do you have in your kitchen? What potentially do you have in your cupboard that we traditionally love or hate? A peculiarly British concoction? I can see it now, bubbling on toast under the grill...

Yes, it's *Marmite*. In any workshop, the group is always divided on the issue of love or hate for this kitchen staple, which for this exercise is perfect. It means you are able to say the word *Marmite* with either adoration or venom, but at least you can say it with passion!

So, to reinforce your ability to find where your chest voice can be found, repeat the above lid-off-the-jar exercise, but as you do so, instead of the original grunt, you can put the image of a Marmite jar in your minds. Whether you are a lover or hater, as you now twist off that lid you can exhort with power and passion the word:

'Marmite!'

That's the chest voice. For key messages.

Now back to your team meeting. Your opening statement is delivered in a richer, stronger, more resonant voice, received by your audience with a touch more authority, a touch more gravitas...

Even a touch of Marmite.

Once more with feeling. Say it from the heart.

A very different scenario now.

Step out of the office for a moment, into a world more personal, a world where you may be touched by tragedy, pain or heartache.

One of the most popular readings at weddings is 1 Corinthians 13:11 which begins: "When I was a child, I talked like a child, I thought like a child, I reasoned like a child." Now, as adults, our lives are tinged with experiences. Experiences that, if we let them, can have an impact on the colour of our voice, enabling us to reach the hearts of our audience with a voice that is often soft, often gentle.

It comes from the heart; resonates with those around us.

That is if we are willing to let that emotion come through, which often we are not.

I recall being on a workshop where we broke into groups to discuss difficult times that involved our families or children, to explore how we use this voice, the heart voice. It didn't take long before we were in buckets of tears from shared experiences...

Now I'm not saying that you should be sharing buckets of tears in the workplace as a matter of course, but sometimes there is the need to talk of painful issues, to empathise with our audience. So let me first of all stress what this is not. It is not talking *about* your feelings, which makes many of us uncomfortable, but speaking *with feeling*.

So why are we so often unwilling to allow our voices to reflect feelings? To reflect emotions?

Yes, often there is the confusion outlined above, our natural reserve about expressing our feelings, but more often than not it is the restraint of being in a professional environment.

I've been there. As a bank manager I was often addressing my fellow professionals, e.g. accountants, solicitors, where there was–or at least I felt there was–a certain expectation of what was considered professional, considered appropriate.

Yet by denying yourself permission to use this voice, you are missing one of the most powerful elements in your presentation; the ability to reach the people in the room on a personal level in a way they will remember. To return again to that quote from the poet Maya Angelou:

'I've learned that people will forget what you said, people will forget what you did, but people will never forget how you made them feel.'

Think of the times you've heard a colleague fired up with enthusiasm after an event or conference where they tell you, "The speaker really got to me / The speaker really spoke from the heart." Why deny yourself the opportunity to add that string to your bow?

So, to find that voice.

Exercise

Again, may I stress that this is not talking *about* your feelings, but talking *with* feeling. It is also not a physical exercise to dig out certain muscles; after all, you know where your heart is!

Instead, as you read this, dig into your memories for moments when you felt your own heart being touched. It may, as on the workshop that I was part of, be something deeply personal, something deeply painful. It may be a companion (human or animal) that you care deeply for, or a cause that always captures your heart. Dwell on those thoughts, those images for a moment, then imagine you are sharing them with someone you care for.

Even better, if you are able to record yourself on a device where you can play back both image and sound, you would find your whole demeanour, not just your voice, was softer. More gentle.

Take this now to your next business presentation, with the knowledge that it is a strength, not a weakness.

You are not being soft, far from it. This is not you stating a fact that anyone can contest or take issue with, it is you using an element of your amazing voice–in a way that other speakers in the room may be reluctant to do for all the reasons above–to reach your audience personally and powerfully.

That's the heart voice. For softer messages.

Think of talking from the heart.

Put your voice there.

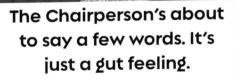

The Chairperson's about to say a few words. It's just a gut feeling.

Now for something completely different.

You're back at the conference. Back in familiar territory for many of us. You've heard some interesting presentations, a brilliant keynote and workshop on public speaking. (I wonder who delivered that...)

It's time for the chair to briefly sum up, to send us all on our way.

If you are in that role, there may be an expectation on you to deliver something brief, yet deep and meaningful.

Or you are running a meeting. Amongst the cacophony of voices around you there is a need to impose a this-is-how-it-is statement to call things to order.

A deeper, more resonant, more imposing voice–no matter the gender–is often associated with the persona of someone more mature, more experienced, carrying more authority. It's about saying this-is-how-it-is more deeply, more resonantly from the gut. This voice is less used than the other conversational voices; a useful addition to the armoury if you know how to access it.

Explore *deep* for a moment. Not so much the content–that's for another book–but matching the voice tone to the message you want to deliver; with maturity, with experience, with authority.

Regardless of gender, the nerves of the moment can affect your intonation. You may have experienced those moments when nerves have caused your voice to squeak up into the stratosphere.

Understanding how to drop your voice–not in volume but in a downward direction towards your gut, not dramatically, but by enough to differ from your normal conversation voice–

can add a touch of authority, a touch of gravitas to your message.

So, to find that voice.

Exercise

Our final exercise. If you are able to, stand up, but clearly not if it is going to make the whole train carriage or office turn to look at you.

- Stand (or sit!) as relaxed, as comfortable as you can. Take a comfortable breath.

- Hum comfortably to yourself. Yes, I did say hum! Imagine you are listening to one of your favourite pieces of music. Hum along.

- Now you're ready to take that vibration down into your gut. Take another breath, begin another hum. Take the sound down through your stomach into your gut, as if the music you are listening to had just swooped to a low note with you accompanying it.

- Staying with that gut feeling, say a final phrase that you would use to close the meeting, or an interjection that you would use to bring the meeting back on track, "What we are going to do now is...." Remember that feeling.

Now you may be thinking that Ges has gone completely bonkers. But the point of this is to find where that voice comes from, so that you can replicate it when you need it.

That is the gut voice, the voice-of-authority in the meeting. Whether you are chairwoman, chairman, chairperson or simply chair.

Conclusion

To recap. You've worked on five voices:

- The voice of silence–powerful, effective

- The head voice–for stories, for interest, for excitement

- The chest voice–for important messages, key statements

- The heart voice–for softer, more personal engagement with your audience

- The gut voice–deeper, richer, with gravitas, with authority

Finally

How do you put this series of voices into practice? How do you move this on from reading words on the page and rehearsal exercises? How do you put this into day-to-day use?

A practical suggestion, mindful of what life is like today. No time to do anything. 4pm request to talk at a 9:30am meeting...

When you are jotting down notes for your next event, next presentation, whether a full-blown, typed-up speech or simply scribbles on the back of an envelope, here's a practical three-step process:

1. Take a moment to think about the impact of your words.

2. Consider what message you want your audience to hear.

3. Against each paragraph or section, pencil the appropriate voice in the margin. Then use it.

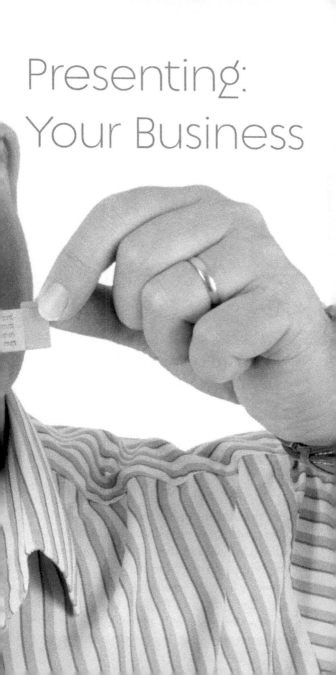

Presenting:
Your Business

I faked a car crash on the M25...

... to avoid going to a networking meeting where I had to stand up to talk about my business.

New Client

Yes, this was the opening greeting from a new client, who gave me permission to quote the words, but—for obvious reasons—not to quote the name. On the morning of a networking event where a speaking slot had been arranged, this was the call that was made after a sleepless night, phone shaking in the hand, faking a motorway smash rather than going to the meeting to speak.

"You're going networking."

What is your reaction to that statement?

Has your stomach just flipped twice, your heart just started racing in reaction to seeing an entry in your diary, a networking event that you have registered for, or accepted an invitation to, yet wish you hadn't?

It may be more of a ***"You're going networking!!!"*** statement, accompanied by triple stomach somersault with heart racing at double speed because it is an instruction that has come from your work environment that you can't get out of, but is the last place on earth that you want to go to.

It's bad enough speaking in public, let alone networking. You're wishing you had thought of the car-crash excuse. Trouble is, it's a bit like the "I have to go to my third cousin's great aunt's grandmother's funeral" ruse for a day off; only so many times you can use it.

You are not alone. A well-known New York Times survey asked people what they most feared. Death came third, after walking into a room full of strangers–yes, that's networking– and speaking in public...

It doesn't have to be like that.

Yes, it's something new, something different. Something that sets off the fight-or-flight feelings together with those familiar symptoms, just as with public speaking. But how did you feel on your first day in a new office? How did you feel on your first day in a new school? How did you feel on your first driving lesson?

Because you had to get through the first day in the office in order to do your job, or wanted to get through your first driving lesson in order to be able to drive, you stuck with it, found ways of dealing with it. Whilst you didn't skip happily into work or school with a grin on your face every day, you probably did a little dance when you picked up the pass certificate after your driving test. You soon put those anxieties to the back of your mind.

You're going networking.

No matter if it is something new, or if you are a seasoned networker, you want to be more effective, you want to be more comfortable, you want more results. In this final section, I'll walk with you through five scenarios, five sets of practical tips drawn from personal–also sometimes painful–experiences.

If you talk to a man in a language he understands, that goes to his head. If you talk to him in his language, that goes to his heart.

Nelson Mandela

It's a 1-2-1. Is this even networking? It's a meeting in the diary. A face-to-face over a coffee, a 1-2-1. The time is booked, the venue is sorted, the agenda is scribbled–well, in your head at least. You know who you are meeting.

But do you?

How often have you exchanged greetings, shaken hands, sat down, then felt slightly at sea as to how to focus the conversation?

Or had that sinking feeling as you're sailing along, realising that your conversation partner is on a different tack? Sunk because you're not sure how to anchor it back into your agenda?

Or time is up; you both have to set sail for your respective horizons. It's time to shake on... What? Not a lot? More small talk than grains of sand on the beach, yet somehow, no connection, no focus, no agenda items covered, let alone ticked off.

How could you have made this more engaging, more productive, more successful?

You knew who you were meeting. Or did you? Yes, you knew the name, who they worked for, something from the initial contact that triggered the meeting, but who were they? What was their style of working? How did they like to be spoken to?

In short, what research could you have undertaken to find out a little more about them? To find a competitive edge? To find a more effective way of building a business relationship?

I'm talking in the past tense here because the moment has gone, the opportunity has been missed, the potential prospect has been downgraded to a mere contact.

Rewind the clock to your preparation for that meeting, add profiling to your pre-meeting tick list, then reorder the coffee.

This may sound like something from a detective series that you are watching, or the latest espionage movie, but adding profiling tools to your meeting preparation could make the difference between the cold coffee-cup dregs of another contact conversation that went nowhere, and the warm, rich aroma of potential business with a prospect.

Starting with those basics, I'm making the assumption that you at least woke up your favourite search engine to look up the person you are about to meet, also hopped onto social media to check out what they are up to, what they are talking about, who is talking about them, together with checking out their company / business sector for latest news.

You could at this point say job done, jacket on, Americano with cream on the side here we come. Many would. But what if you could delve deeper? Have an overview of their personality? Have an understanding of what motivates them?

How much richer could the conversation be if you were equipped to speak to them in a style which they preferred?

What if you could discover your coffee conversation client's personality ahead of the meeting? What if you could gain an insight into their behaviour, their preferred conversation style before anyone said a word?

Profiling tools help here. Profiling tools / personality platforms feel like they should meet you wearing a homburg hat, swathed in swirling mist under the station clock with a red rose in the buttonhole for identification.

Spooky or not, tools such as these help you understand your client–also yourself!

Restart the clock. You have researched, you have profiled, you have for good measure thrown in a search at Companies House for present and past directorships.

The coffee arrives. Warm, welcoming, matching your greeting to your companion, already in a style that makes them feel comfortable. This is no longer merely a meeting in the diary, no longer an unachievable agenda; this is 1-2-1 networking.

Job done, jackets off; Americanos with cream on the side ordered.

You now really do know who you are meeting. You are talking in their language, going to their heart, building a business relationship.

Bangers, beans and bacon...

... with black pudding (optional) on the side...

Scaling up from 1-2-1 meetings, you're now at a business breakfast, staple diet of the networking scene with standard fare for both the consumables and the meeting content. You set the alarm clock, you rose early, arrived on time. You've paid your membership fee, been ticked off the list, met all the requirements.

But in a cup of coffee plus a plate of breakfast's time, you, together with the others in the room, will be expected to stand up, to speak about your business. Whether it's a 60-second round, a 40-second round, or a more informal session, this is your opportunity to engage your audience.

This is your moment, your chance to catch someone's interest in what you can do for them, whether in or through the room.

But how have you prepared? What can you do to help ensure this is not simply another car crash of a meeting (other than nearly crashing the car on the way to the meeting as you frantically scrabbled for a few words to say this morning)?

Another less than memorable meeting where no one really remembers a word that you said? You've paid to be there; what can you do to help make it worthwhile?

What you can do is ask yourself what's your *you* count?

Here's a compilation networking statement garnered from many, many meetings over the years. I promise not attributable to anyone I know:

"Good Morning. I'm Arbuthnot Babblemore. I'm Managing Director of Woefully Wretched Widgets Ltd. We were established in 1957, we have recently moved to our new offices in Newtown and our in-house team of woeful consultants together with our wretched partners in three major cities provide first-class woefully wretched widget services to our clients across the world. Our woefully wretched widgets come in all standard sizes."

I / we / our count ten, *you* count zero.

Attend any event, from networking to internal meeting where attendees have to stand up or speak in turn around the table, sometimes both, this pattern of introduction will be fairly standard.

How much of Arbuthnot's message have you taken on board? How many of you will be seeking out Arbuthnot for a coffee after the meeting to continue the conversation?

Arbuthnot finishes his introduction then sits down. You may hold a snapshot of his business in your mind for a split second, at least until the next introduction begins. But unless there was something that specifically caught your attention because it was relevant to you, your business, or someone that you know, the chances are that by the time a few more people have spoken you will have difficulty recalling even his name, let alone his business. Even if it is Arbuthnot.

I / we / our count ten, you count zero. It's the *yous* that count, as your audience's interest in you as a speaker is, well, also zero.

An audience is not interested in the speaker; an audience is interested in what the speaker can do for them. At your networking event, your audience, even for a brief introduction, is not interested in you or your business; they are interested in what you or your business can do for them.

So reverse the polarity of your presentation; switch the focus from all about you to all about them. Using a case study, using an example, building a story into your introduction that your audience can understand, can identify with, will resonate with your listeners. Will help you be remembered.

To adapt an age-old adage, it's not about me, it's about you.

You're off to a conference!
Mind the elevators.

"It was a dark and stormy night..."

It was, it really was. Appropriately dark, gloomy atmospheric conditions for one of the most excruciatingly awkward conversations—if you could call it a conversation—from financial services days. Having eagerly targeted, traced, then tied down a prospect for an appointment, we met one evening at his home.

The doorbell died in the distance, the key scraped in the lock, the heavy door creaked open on its hinges. To say he welcomed me over the threshold would be a misrepresentation; more accurate to say he at least didn't set the dogs on me as permission was given to enter.

Ushered into a large room, the small chair in one corner was indicated as the chosen destination. My reluctant host then proceeded to a larger, more comfortable chair in the diagonally opposite corner of this very large room, sat down, legs crossed, arms folded, indicating I should begin.

Hardly a word had been uttered until this point. After spluttering through bank manager spiel as to all the amazing services we offered, the meeting was clearly over. I returned to my car, returned to home. We never spoke again.

Why this painfully personal story?

The parallel here is the conference ambush. Not quite so dramatic, but you've been there, I've been there, we've all been there. Hardly in the door when you're met with an eager outstretched hand, a business card waved under your nose. An elevator pitch spiel about their business.

Recognise that profile? Is that / has that been you, cards in hand, elevator pitch spiel at the ready? Hands up, I've done it.

How can you avoid being the provocateur, luring your target into a conference ambush? How can you instead open a more engaging conversation more likely to be of mutual benefit? What is the oft-maligned elevator pitch? How can you turn it to your advantage?

One definition (amongst many) is:

"A brief, persuasive speech that you use to spark interest in what your organisation does. You can also use them to create interest in a project, idea or product, or in yourself. A good elevator pitch should last no longer than an elevator ride of 20 to 30 seconds."

Hence the name, of course with many variations, although I'll lay odds neither you or I have delivered a pitch whilst in an elevator.... I did once have an odd conversation in an elevator whilst in Chicago, but that's another story for another time; ask me when we meet.

As an aside, one of my colleagues recently had an escalator conversation, where the other party was running late for a train. The only face-to-face space was the time from the foot to the top of the station escalator... Again, that's a story for another time.

So back to your conference. Back to the obvious. Two individuals approach you, one after the other. Both, to be fair, equally warm, equally smiling.

One launches into patter about what they do, what services they offer, what they can do for you.

The other greets you, asks about *you*, asks about *your* business, what *your* business does.

With whom are you more likely to continue the conversation?

Yes, of course. As the sunlight of sensibility streams over your shoulder though the stained glass window of reasoning in your chapel of contentment whilst you sit comfortably in the armchair reading this, the answer is obvious.

But what do *you* do? What's *your* approach? How do *you* make new acquaintances at a conference?

No matter where you are on the scales of experience, you can improve. Whether you are learning, still refining or honing the skill of managing conference conversations, here's a three-step approach to support you:

- What is the focus of the event / conference? What are the news stories? What are the social media conversations? Read, research, be ready to engage.

- What is happening in the world of the person you are talking to? If you have done your research on the conference attendees list, the chances are there will be particular names who fit your profile of a potentially good fit to have a conversation with. Don't leave it to chance; go one step further than many of your competitors. Spend a few minutes on the hot topics, the hot buttons for that person, their business.

- Last, but not least, don't ask "What do you do?" Instead ask, "What's your expertise?"

You may be surprised at the responses you receive to that last open question. You have just opened the door to a world beyond their business, given permission for a response that transcends the conference. A response that invites more personal detail; a charity role, a trusteeship, a skill, a hobby... A response that opens the door to a deeper, richer exchange.

More importantly, you have avoided the elevator pitch trap altogether, instead made the conversation a more personal one.

Again, made it not all about me, but about you.

All the world's a stage

As You Like It, Act II, Scene VII
William Shakespeare

And you're on it! You've scaled up; all that networking, all those engaging conversations have paid dividends. Now you are on stage. A stage that may be a networking event where you are the speaker for that meeting. A business expo where you are one of the keynote speakers or one of the presenters in the seminar theatres. One of the speakers during the course of the company conference.

It is your opportunity to speak 1-2-many instead of 1-2-1. You are rehearsed; techniques, voice tones, even your slides *(do you even need slides?)* have been through many iterations. From a presentation point of view, you are about to nail it.

But what's the point of you being there in the first place? What about the networking side of your speaking slot? What else can you do to reach out, make personal contact with the individuals in your audience, improve the chances of building business relationships, improve the chances of doing business?

Think for a moment about the ability of good comedians to ask members of the audience what they do for a living, then come up with brilliant one-liners, apparently off the cuff, that have the audience in stitches of laughter.

The trick of their trade is these are not off the cuff. Not by happenchance. The good comedian will have researched a range of roles, a range of occupations, then rehearsed a couple of seemingly instantaneous responses to each. Result? The audience member is made to feel special (or not, depending on the response!), a laugh is achieved, job done.

Now, I'm not suggesting that you should consider taking the role of stand-up comedian at your events (although I do know good speakers who regard this as excellent training). But I am suggesting that taking a leaf out of their preparation book would be to your advantage.

Here's a three-step preparation plan:

- Who is in your audience? Talk to attendees / delegates beforehand, solicit their views on the topic. If appropriate, obtain their permission beforehand to refer to that conversation in your talk. Being able to include, "As Lois was saying earlier," during the course of your presentation achieves several objectives:

- It briefly switches the focus from you to your audience, helping to make your speech about your audience, not about you

- It makes Lois feel a bit special. No matter what status we have in life, to have a shout-out in the room elevates us for a moment

- It pretty well guarantees that Lois will want to come up to thank you, to have that coffee / drink in the bar with you afterwards!

- What businesses are in the audience? What are their industries? What are their sectors? What are their buzz words? By tailoring your content, your language to resonate with the people in the room you begin to build a rapport from the stage, further building your chances of a worthwhile conversation afterwards

- What were the points made by the previous speakers? What messages did they leave in the room? Referring back, interweaving relevant points made on that same stage in earlier presentations helps reinforce the message you are delivering, again building rapport and your credibility with your audience

All the world's a stage, and you are on it. Working on the skills, the techniques to be a good speaker is half the job. The other half is developing the networking skills that build relationships that build business.

You've worked hard to earn the right to be on that stage; now be as effective after the event.

116

It's a wrap... or is it?

You're done. Finished. Finito. Fini. The stage
is empty, the room a sea of empty coffee cups,
the earlier crescendo of conference chatter
now a diminuendo as voices turn to the topics
of train times, arranging taxis. Transport
home is the new priority.

You're done.

Or are you?

How many times have you begun a conversation
at an event, exchanged business cards, parted
with a warm handshake, a cheery smile, then
ne'er spoke again?

How many times have you returned home after
an event, emptied a pile of business cards on
the desk? Then picked them up a few days
later whilst struggling to remember who they
were or what the conversation was about?

How many times have you turned from the
departing conversation, with the other party's
words ringing in your ears, "I'll be in touch!"
Then heard nothing?

As a speaker, your job is not done until you
are in the car, on the train or on the plane
heading for home. Until then you remain on

stage as your audience still expects to be able to continue the conversation that you started, still expects to continue the relationship with the person they met when in their seats.

As a speaker *and a networker*, your job is not done until you have followed up on those contacts. Begun the process of turning those contacts into business relationships.

Again, a straightforward three-step process:

- If you are unable to immediately process the business cards, the odd notes on napkins (we've all done it...), the jottings on odd pieces of literature, at least add a couple of keyword reminders–s*eminar room, day 1, dark hair*–to help avoid that blank memory moment a few days later.

- Record the detail. In bank manager days we worked off paper files (yes, I know...), with client details summarised on index cards. I can still see them in my mind's eye now; a riot of colours with snippets of information recorded in different inks, all the better to inform the next conversation. Today's equivalent is your CRM (Customer Relationship Management) system, with low-cost, cloud-based solutions readily available.

- Then follow up, follow up, follow up. Social media contact, warm non-salesy email, good old-fashioned phone call, all with a hook for the next contact.

Now you are not the one that says, "I'll be in touch," yet does nothing; now you are the one that builds on your speaking and networking skills to build business relationships.

Now your job is done; now it's a wrap.

Or is it?

"This is about the principle of marginal gains, not dramatic changes or Damascene revelations. By tweaking the performance of each element of your speaking, with practice and rehearsal you build your skills, build yourself into a more effective speaker."

What next for you? What will you work on to build yourself into an even more effective speaker?

Acknowledgements

Jim Durant, English teacher at Tiffin School, who inspired in me a love of language that I did not fully appreciate for many years. *Miss Wilson*, personnel manager, unknowingly the catalyst for commencing my speaking career in national public speaking competitions. *Bob King*, bank boss, who farsightedly put me through a professional radio broadcasting course. *Steve Kavanagh*, CEO, who taught me more about business than any course ever could. *Jon Pullinger*, who re-introduced me to the world of choral music, re-awakening my love of singing. *Peter Wilford*, career coach, whose apposite questions sparked the realisation of a nascent role in life. *Judy Apps*, fellow singer, inspirational author, speaker and voice coach, in whose footsteps I follow. *Richard Hagen*, publisher with a difference. And *Martyn Pentecost*, book coach supreme, who facilitated the seemingly magical transformation of a pile of workshop notes into a publication that I can take pride in.

My thanks to you all.

About Ges

By now you should already know me quite well. Maybe too well. After all, I've been your embarrassment sponge throughout your first steps as a confident, compelling and convincing presenter.

If you want to know even more about me or wish to continue your transformation into a dynamic, dazzling and dreamy presenter, here is everything you need...

I've been a bank manager (after working my way up from tea boy) and business development manager in large corporates and SMEs. My passion for speaking and presenting began with work, though I guess I've always loved performing as music and singing has always been in my soul.

Now I get to combine my business expertise with my passion for public speaking and presenting by delivering keynotes for large organisations or by emceeing their events. Afterwards, I often find myself running workshops for leaders, managers and teams within these organisations. I also coach executives; tailored presentation training, frequently at the last minute.

And of course, I indulge my love for singing as much as I possibly can amongst the voices of the magnificent Dorking Choral Society.

If you are looking for a confident, compelling and convincing speaker, coach or MC, you already know who to contact. All you need now is my phone number. It is good to talk; coffee together is even better...

+44 (0) 794 108 3722

ges.ray@speakinginpublic.info

http://www.linkedin.com/in/gesray

www.speakinginpublic.info

Online courses and events:

www.speakperformance.online

Other books from mPowr Publishing

Your Slides Suck!

David Henson

ISBN—978-1-907282-78-2

The book for all speakers! How to make engaging, empowering and effective PowerPoint presentations.

How to Make a Confident and Memorable Wedding Speech

Graham Le-Gall

ISBN—978-1-907282-82-9

For those who find themselves in the honoured and terrifying position of speaking on the big day.

Mission: Leadership

Ben Morton

ISBN—978-1-907282-71-3

For mangers, coaches and leaders. How to create and support strong teams by encouraging heroes, liberating victims and challenging the villains in your workplace.

Hire Power
John Wallace
ISBN—978-1-907282-83-6
For HR specialists and senior management. How to leverage strategic resourcing to create a competitive advantage.

Storyselling
Martyn Pentecost
ISBN—978-1-907282-59-1
For those who understand that stories are the most powerful tool for persuasion and promotion. Strategy, techniques and tactics that will revolutionise your marketing approach and your entire business.

From the Publisher's Guide Series

The Heist:
Cracking the Marketing Code
ISBN—978-1-907282-24-9
For those who want to understand how to use books as a powerful element of their marketing mix. The key elements required for a powerful strategy.